Haverhill Public Library
Founded 1874
Haverhill, Massachusetts

SOCRATES

ANCIENT GREEK IN SEARCH OF TRUTH

SPECIAL LIVES IN HISTORY THAT BECOME

Signature LIVES

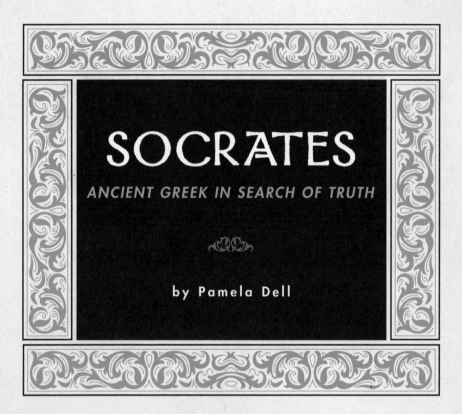

SOCRATES

ANCIENT GREEK IN SEARCH OF TRUTH

by Pamela Dell

Content Adviser: Debra Nails, Ph.D.,
Department of Philosophy,
Michigan State University

Reading Adviser: Rosemary G. Palmer, Ph.D.,
Department of Literacy, College of Education,
Boise State University

COMPASS POINT BOOKS  MINNEAPOLIS, MINNESOTA

Compass Point Books
3109 West 50th Street, #115
Minneapolis, MN 55410

Visit Compass Point Books on the Internet at *www.compasspointbooks.com*
or e-mail your request to *custserv@compasspointbooks.com*

Editor: Shelly Lyons
Page Production: Blue Tricycle
Photo Researcher: Svetlana Zhurkin
Cartographer: XNR Productions, Inc.
Library Consultant: Kathleen Baxter

Art Director: Jaime Martens
Creative Director: Keith Griffin
Editorial Director: Carol Jones
Managing Editor: Catherine Neitge

Library of Congress Cataloging-in-Publication Data
Dell, Pamela.
  Socrates: ancient Greek in search of truth / by Pamela Dell.
     p. cm.—(Signature lives)
  Includes bibliographical references and index.
  ISBN-13: 978-0-7565-1874-5 (hardcover)
  ISBN-10: 0-7565-1874-1 (hardcover)
  1. Socrates. I. Title. II. Series.
  B316.D46 2006
  183'.2—dc22   2006005405

ANCIENT GREECE

After the fall of Troy around 1180 B.C. in the Trojan War, soldiers returned to a Greece mired in famine and economic collapse. It was a time for rebuilding. Greece underwent a political and cultural transformation 400 years after the war with the transition to independent city-states and the establishment of the Olympics. Athens became the hub for developments in architecture, art, science, and philosophy. In about 460 B.C., ancient Greece entered its golden age, one that would produce the establishment of democracy, the beginnings of university study, great strides in medicine and science, architectural advancements, and the creation of plays and epic poems that are still enjoyed today.

Table of Contents

1 A Man on Trial

❧⟨∽⟩❧

It was springtime in the year 399 B.C., and the citizens' court of Athens was jam-packed. The jury alone numbered 501 members. All of them were men over the age of 30, all legally recognized Athenian citizens chosen by lottery.

Spectators as well as the jury filled the courtroom that morning. Many were lifelong friends of the defendant. Others were his bitter enemies. All were there to witness the one-day trial of Socrates, a famous man throughout Athens.

Given the reputation of Socrates and the crimes he was charged with, the trial was an event few in Athens wanted to miss. The morning began with the reading of the charges against the defendant. Both sides were riveted as they waited for what was to

The ancient Greek philosopher Socrates was charged with and put on trial for impiety and corrupting the youth of Athens.

Ideal View of the City of Athens in Antiquity, by 19th-century painter and architect Leo von Klenze

come. One side hoped to see Socrates win another argument right before their eyes. The other side hoped he would soon be convicted.

Athenian law required those who brought charges to try their own cases. There were three accusers. The youngest of them—a poet with long hair, a scruffy beard, and a hawklike beak of a nose—was serving as the main prosecutor. His name was Meletus. The other two were Lycon, an orator, or speech giver, and Anytus, a powerful political leader. Socrates—a short, thick-bodied 70-year-old man with bulging eyes, thick lips, and a flat pug nose—stood before his accusers. He was accused of impiety, or refusing to accept the

Athenian gods. The second charge was corrupting the youth by spreading his beliefs to them. Socrates argued that he was guilty of neither offense.

When the accusers finished their proceedings in court, Socrates was given time to speak:

> *I don't know, men of Athens, how you were affected by my accusers. As for me, I was almost carried away by them, they spoke so persuasively. And yet almost nothing they said is true. ... You see, many people have been accusing me in front of you for very many years now—and nothing they say is true.*

After hours of arguing his own defense, Socrates ended his speech with a few simple words: "I turn it over to you and to the god to judge me in whatever way will be best for me and for yourselves."

It was time for the jurors to make their judgment. To do so, they would think about what they had heard without leaving the room or discussing the matter among themselves. A simple majority vote would determine the outcome.

After a long day in court, the trial was over. By a vote of 361-140, Socrates was condemned to death. He was sentenced to die in a painless and dignified way by voluntarily drinking a cup of the deadly poison hemlock. When he received the sentence, Socrates gave a long speech. He told the people in court, "And

now I take my leave, convicted by you of a capital crime, whereas they stand forever convicted by the truth of wickedness and injustice."

Socrates had spent his life seeking wisdom and striving to understand the difference between right and wrong. He had exposed the ignorance of men who thought they were filled with knowledge. His greatest goal had always been to act as a good and virtuous person and to encourage others to do the same. His followers believed Socrates had the greatest mind in all of Greece, and they did not want to lose him.

As Socrates' closest circle of friends filed out of the Athens law court, deeply troubled, one question loomed large: Would Socrates accept the sentence that had been dealt to him and down the drink of death? Or, as they hoped, would he find some means to escape his fate? ❧

2 FORTUNATE BEGINNINGS

❧✦❧

In southeastern Europe lies a land of sun-baked hills, gnarled olive trees, and ancient ruins. Surrounding this land on three sides are glittering seas dotted with 2,000 islands. This place is called Greece, a country only about as big as the state of Alabama. But despite its small size, Greece has given the world some of its greatest cultural gifts.

The ancient Greeks are especially famous for one important reason. They brought to the Western world the tradition of studying the nature of reality and the truths that underlie all knowledge. The Greeks called this search for truth *philosophia*, or in English, "philosophy," meaning the love of wisdom.

Ancient writings tell us that Socrates was born in 469 B.C. in the tiny political district of Alopece in

Ancient Athens was a booming city-state full of marvelous architecture, art, and clever minds.

The Olympic Games, democracy, and the study of philosophy were three of the most enduring things that came from ancient Greece. But many other common aspects of culture originated there as well. The ancient Greeks were pioneers in what became modern medicine, and they were the first to discover classical proportion—the basis of art and architecture. Some Greeks understood the principles of the camera and observed the effects of light passing through a pinhole. The dramatic forms of comedy and tragedy both originated in ancient Greece, as did the epic poetry associated with Homer. Today, there are few places in the world where the influence of ancient Greek civilization has not been felt.

Athens long before there was a country called Greece.

Athens' population was about 500,000 at the time of Socrates' birth. The region where Athens was and still is located is called Attica. It is a dry, hilly region of eastern Greece.

Socrates' father, Sophroniscus, was a stonecutter. Some historical writings suggest that Socrates also learned his father's trade. Socrates' mother, Phaenarete, worked as a midwife, delivering babies.

By custom, after a birth, the baby's father or guardian would decide whether or not the infant was worth keeping. If he decided the baby should not be kept, the baby would be exposed—placed in an urn and left in a sacred area away from habitation to die or to be rescued.

Like all babies who were not abandoned, Socrates probably went through traditional religious rites. His father would have carried him around the hearth when he was

5 days old, a ritual that formally admitted him into his family. At 10 days old, he would have received his name. In his first year, Sophroniscus also would have introduced Socrates into the family's regional hereditary society, called a *phratry*, and been responsible for teaching him all about the local social customs of the city.

In the early fifth century B.C., Athens was a dramatic place. There, the sound of war drums was almost continual. For hundreds of years, the Persian Empire to the east had been waging war against various Greek-speaking provinces, or city-states. At that time, the city-states had not yet united into a single

The Persian Wars lasted 51 years, from 500 to 449 B.C.

country called Greece. The territory was known as Hellas and its people as Hellenes. Each city-state had its own laws and government. It was one region against another, with alliances formed and broken according to need.

The empire of Persia controlled some of the city-states. Other city-states had banded together to

Ancient Greece consisted of many city-states, and its boundaries reached beyond those of present-day Greece.

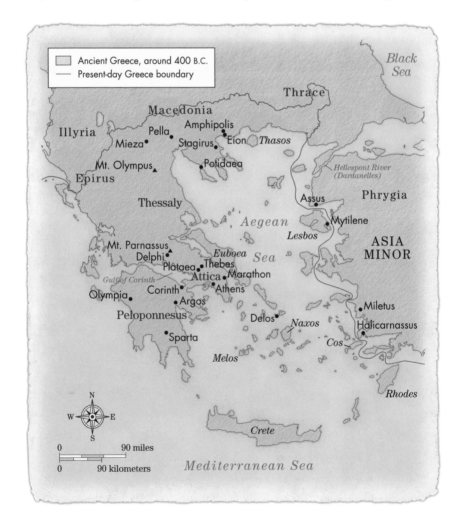

defend themselves against the Persians. But conflict was constant throughout the region, and the balance of power continually shifted.

In 480 B.C., Persian armies destroyed Athens. By the time of Socrates' birth 11 years later, the city had done much to rebuild. It had become the leading power among the other nearby city-states. By 469, Athens was the region's center of dramatic festivals, religion, and politics.

On a hill towering over Athens sat the Acropolis, a Greek word that means "the high city." Most Hellenic cities had an acropolis, which served as a fort in times of war.

At the time of Socrates' birth, literacy had been commonplace in Athens for at least 50 years. By the time he was 6 or 7 years old, Socrates was no doubt attending one of the many elementary schools in the city. The Hellenes felt it was important to train boys intellectually and physically, mainly to prepare them for war.

At school, Socrates would have learned to read, write, and do arithmetic, often from slaves who served as teachers. Male students also participated in sports like wrestling, gymnastics, and track. In addition to their regular education, many young men also learned the art of speech-giving and persuasive argument, which were useful in both the courts and the citizen Assembly. Athens had no elected officials,

Young Greek men partici- pated in physi- cal education as part of their schooling.

except for military generals, so much depended on a man's ability to sway other men with words.

As he approached the age of 18, Socrates became eligible to become an Athenian citizen. Only men who had been born of two Athenian parents could qualify for citizenship. To become a citizen, Socrates would first have been formally presented by his father to the members of the family's tribe in Alopece. After an examination, his name would be added to the roll of Athenian citizens.

As a citizen, Socrates would be eligible for spe- cific privileges and responsibilities within the state. The first responsibility was a required two-year training in Athens' militia. Like other Athenian boys, Socrates had prepared for the military since childhood by engaging in wrestling, running, and other sports. At the age of 30, he would have even more privileges of citizenship, including the right to vote for or against any legal measures citizens proposed. He would also be able to propose his own legal measures. By tradition, like most young Athenian men, he probably lived at home until this time.

When Socrates' father, Sophroniscus, died, Athenian law made Socrates his mother's legal guardian. She would have needed his permission to remarry and was required to remarry if he demanded it. Whatever the reason, she remarried and gave Socrates a half-brother, Patrocles.

Although his family was not wealthy, they were well-respected, giving Socrates access to the many intellectual riches of Athens. Living in that city in the fifth century B.C. was, for him, a case of being in the right place at the right time. Many great thinkers were Athenian citizens. And as the most powerful city-state in the Hellenic world, Athens drew many more from other places. At first, Socrates was eager to absorb the teachings of these learned men. But he would soon find he had a mind of his own. ℀

3 THE BIRTH OF PHILOSOPHY

Chapter

❦❦❦

Every day the sun moved from one side of the sky to the other. Every evening that ball of fire would sink, and the stars would appear, scattered across the blackness. The moon changed its shape as the nights passed. Insects crawled and flew. Flowers and trees sprouted from small seeds. Women gave birth.

As a boy, Socrates was surely eager to find out how the universe and all the things in it came to exist. He wanted to know why the world operated as it did. To find the answers to these questions, Socrates needed wise teachers.

The Athens of Socrates' youth and young adulthood was full of people concerned with what was called the science of nature, or natural philosophy. Many of these people were natives of Athens.

Others were modern thinkers who had been born elsewhere but had come to Athens because of its reputation as the center of culture. These natural philosophers put forth their theories to explain the workings of the external world: what its parts consisted of, how natural phenomena worked, and how each part fit together with the rest. Some of them gave public lectures. They also provided structured classes to students who could afford to pay fees.

Coming from a family of modest means, Socrates had little opportunity for formal training. But with his intense intellectual curiosity, he was attracted to the teachings of many of the day's leading thinkers. As he grew older, he began questioning these thinkers and learning as much as he could about their theories.

One of the most famous of these was Anaxagoras. Socrates first became aware of him when he heard someone reading Anaxagoras' writings aloud and bought the scroll for himself.

Socrates already knew much about astronomy and geometry, and he also knew something about music and poetry. From

> *Anaxagoras stood out in Athens because his ideas were so new and radical. According to his teachings, the sun was a ball of burning-hot iron hanging in the sky. He believed that the moon was made of earth and that houses, hills, and gullies existed there. Later in his life, Anaxagoras was tried in court for atheism, his belief that there was no God. He ended up in prison. But he did have one thing fairly accurate. He taught that the moon reflected the sun's light.*

The Greek philosopher Anaxagoras

Anaxagoras and others, he absorbed the modern concepts of natural science that were whirling around Athens. According to Plato, a student of Socrates', one of Socrates' most influential role models was a Greek priestess named Diotima of Mantinea, a woman he met when he was about 30. Plato said Diotima passed on wisdom about love to Socrates.

Diotima taught Socrates that love changes in its nature as a person grows from youth to adulthood. The first stirrings of love, she said, come from the appreciation of physical beauty. Then, as a person matures, he or she becomes more able to see the beauty in people who don't fit the ideal of physical perfection. When this happens, a deeper sense of love and beauty sets in—an appreciation for inner beauty, or the beauty of the soul.

These ideas about love may have appealed to Socrates, changing the way he looked at the world and those around him. But for him, the science of nature was another story. Although he had been excited about the subject at first, Socrates noticed that the theories of those who studied and taught natural philosophy dealt only with what exists and how it originated. One such philosopher thought that life began in the heated mud of the sea and that land creatures such as human beings emerged later from a kind of bark on the sea creatures. But to Socrates, these odd and various explanations were not the least bit satisfying. Everyone had a different explanation for how things occurred. But none of these explanations could be proved.

When it came to the mysteries of the physical universe, these men of supposedly great learning had no answers to the one question that Socrates considered most crucial: How should a person live?

Socrates turned his attention to examining those things he felt were truly useful. The questions that began to interest him as he grew into adulthood had to do with the human mind and spirit. He wanted to investigate human actions. He wanted to understand what happiness and courage were and what made a person good or bad. And he wanted to figure out how a person could achieve moral excellence.

This revolutionary shift in Socrates' attention was a turning point for philosophy itself. Before Socrates,

Ancient Greeks had open-air discussions on philosophy and science.

Western philosophers had been gazing outward at the world in search of answers. Now, with the questions of this one man, the people around him began to look at the world differently. Philosophy became a field of study that sought to answer how it was best to live and how others should be treated.

One other major event also helped send Socrates on his quest for truth. North of Athens, on the south side of Mount Parnassus, was Delphi, the site of a temple dedicated to the Greek god Apollo. The temple housed the famous Oracle of Delphi. An oracle

Greeks consulted the Oracle of Delphi for advice.

was a priest or priestess whose job was to transmit advice and wisdom from the gods. In Socrates' time, the priestess at Delphi, sometimes called the Sybil, was the most powerful of any oracle anywhere. People came from as far away as Egypt to seek advice before dealing with any important matter.

One of those visitors to Delphi was a man by the name of Chaerephon, a tall, skinny, rather creepy-looking man. Chaerephon was a good friend of Socrates' and had been since both were boys. At Delphi, Chaerephon asked the oracle if anyone was wiser than Socrates. The answer to this question would send Socrates on a path that would determine the rest of his life.

The Sybil told Chaerephon that no one was wiser than Socrates.

Delphi, the spiritual center of all Hellas, was also considered to be the omphalos, or "navel," of the world. Inscribed on the temple at Delphi are the words "Know Thyself." The job of the Delphic Sybil was sometimes to help humanity with this quest. To receive her messages from the gods, the Sybil would sit on a rock and breathe in the vapors that rose from the sacred area. Soon her words would flow, giving warnings, messages, or instructions. Today, geologists believe that the oracle might have been inhaling methane or ethylene, narcotic gases that may cause hallucinations.

4 PEACE, WAR, AND PLAGUE

In 460 B.C., an Athenian named Pericles ordered changes in Athens. These changes ushered in what became known as Athens' Golden Age, or the Golden Age of Pericles. Under Pericles' guidance, Athens' reputation as the richest center of culture in the Hellenic world became even greater. Poets, playwrights, and philosophers made Athens a city of ideas. It was the ideal atmosphere for Socrates as he grew from a boy into a young man.

This lively intellectual environment was not the only advantage to the young Socrates. From the time he was a child, he believed he had a *daimon,* or guiding spirit. In Plato's writings, Socrates says:

A divine and daimonic thing comes to me. … It's something that began happening to me in childhood: a sort of voice comes, which, whenever it does come, always holds me back from what I'm about to do but never urges me forward.

One of Pericles' most important projects was the restoration of the temple dedicated to Athena on Athens' Acropolis in 449 B.C. Each city-state had its own protecting deity, and Athena, the virgin goddess of war, was the one who watched over Athens, her namesake. This new shrine to Athena was a way of giving thanks for Athens' survival of the Persian Wars of the late sixth and early fifth centuries B.C. Pericles ensured that the shrine would be magnificent. Today, what remains of that beautiful building, called the Parthenon, is hailed internationally as one of the world's most important historic monuments.

Although the English word *demon* has its roots in this Greek word, daimons in Socrates' time were not considered bad. They were thought to be more like beings that existed between the realms of human beings and the gods. Some daimons, like the one Socrates described, were believed to be good. Today, what Socrates called his daimon might be known as good intuition. Socrates considered his ability to hear the voice of his daimon a kind of divine madness. But if the young philosopher-to-be was hearing voices, they were not making him crazy. When the daimon spoke, it kept him from doing something. Socrates trusted completely in his daimon and followed its direction throughout his life.

A fresco from the Assemblée Nationale in Paris, France, shows Socrates and his daimon.

The Golden Age was not without its conflicts, though. Sparta, another city-state, had long
been one of Athens' greatest rivals. A peace treaty
between Athens and Sparta lasted 14 years, from 445
to 431 B.C. Then fighting broke out between them,
marking the beginning of the Peloponnesian War.
This war would continue until 404. One of the initial
conflicts of this war was the Battle of Potidaea in 431.
One of the soldiers defending Athens in the battle
and later siege at Potidaea was Socrates.

The rumblings of unrest in Potidaea, a colony

150 miles (240 kilometers) north of Athens, had begun in 432, when Socrates was 37 years old. Potidaea was an unwilling part of the Athenian Empire. Athens feared that the colony's loyalty was turning to Corinth, an ally of Sparta. When the Potidaean people rose up in rebellion, Athens' soldiers swept in by sea and land—Socrates among them—and, after a siege of nearly three years, ended the revolt.

Socrates served as a hoplite, or heavily-armed foot soldier, in a regiment. According to historians, his service was always courageous and honorable. He did not mind sacrifice, either. Plato describes the famous general Alcibiades, who said that at times when Socrates didn't have shoes or a coat, he would walk for miles without complaining, even in winter.

Fighting as a hoplite was a dangerous business. Rows of soldiers went running into the enemy lines, battling face to face. Because the hoplites provided their own equipment, there was no standard uniform. Enemies were hard to distinguish.But Socrates' daimon had not advised him to stay away. Not only was Socrates not injured in that early battle at Potidaea, but he distinguished himself. Disregarding his own safety, Socrates saved the life of Alcibiades, then a handsome, young soldier who had become his friend and admirer. When Socrates was commended for his bravery in this heroic mission, he modestly insisted that Alcibiades be honored instead.

During the Peloponnesian War, Socrates saw combat at least two more times—at the Battle of Delium seven years later, serving alongside Alcibiades, and then at Amphipolis in 422 B.C.

Socrates saved Alcibiades at the Battle of Potidaea.

A loss at Amphipolis did not improve morale. From that point on, Athens began to lose its position as the supreme sea power in Hellas. The city would spend nearly the next 20 years in a slow decline as it lost one battle after another.

In 430 B.C., when Socrates was 39 years old, a four-year plague broke out in the city. The Spartans had burned the crops, so the people all crowded in

*An ancient
Greek hoplite*

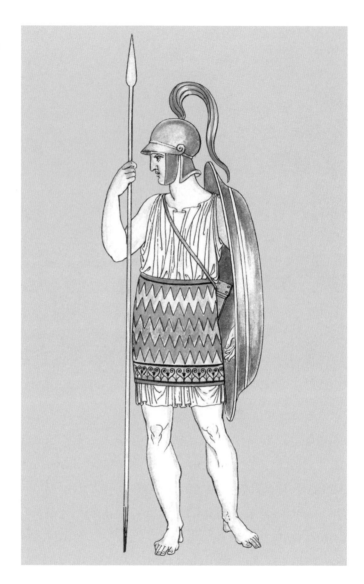

behind the city's walls. When the epidemic struck
Athens, brought in by rat-infested grain shipments, it
turned the city into a landscape of horror and chaos.

The plague of Athens wiped out as much as

one-third of the population. Many believed that the plague was a sign that the gods favored Sparta and were displeased with Athens. Losing all hope, people spent money wildly and carelessly, and every sort of crime broke out. Among those who perished during the plague were Athens' most influential citizen, Pericles, and his two eldest sons. Thousands of civilians died, and the citizen militia lost many officers and troops.

Throughout the wars and the horrors of the plague, Socrates survived. The absence of virtue and piety in his beloved city may have been harder for him to bear than the sight of deadly disease. By this time, Socrates had already begun his quest to understand virtue and to inspire excellence in those around him.

The gods seemed to be watching over him, or perhaps his daimon had kept him from danger. Now, the words of the Oracle of Delphi were guiding his steps. Socrates believed he was meant to leave the life of a soldier and take on a higher mission. To fulfill this divine calling, he would have to use his mind.

> *Today, there are many theories about what the plague may have been. Its symptoms were ghastly. According to the ancient Greek historian Thucydides, it began with burning red eyes, headache, and then bleeding from the mouth. Many other terrible physical conditions followed. People broke out in skin ulcers and boils. They experienced violent stomach pain and vomiting. The disease took about a week to run its course and usually ended in death.*

5 A MISSION FROM APOLLO

❧

Socrates had focused on questions concerning right and wrong, or ethics, since he had given up on natural science. But when he learned that the Oracle of Delphi had declared him the wisest of all, he was puzzled. Socrates believed the god Apollo had sent him a message. But it was a strange one. Socrates asked:

> *What can the god be saying? What does his riddle mean? For I'm only too aware that I've no claim to be wise in anything either great or small. What can he mean, then, by saying that I'm wisest?*

For a long time, Socrates could not understand the meaning of the oracle's answer. Hoping to figure it out, he began questioning many public figures who

The Greek god Apollo is depicted in the marble Roman sculpture Apollo of Belvedere. *It is a copy of a bronze Greek sculpture that was made between 320 and 350* B.C.

had a reputation for being highly knowledgeable citizens. But as he questioned each of them, often while others listened, it became obvious that these men knew little after all.

After questioning the first man, Socrates thought to himself:

I'm wiser than that person. For it's likely that neither of us knows anything fine and good, but he thinks he knows something he doesn't know, whereas I, since I don't in fact know, don't think that I do either. At any rate, it seems that I'm wiser than he in just this one small way: that what I don't know, I don't think I know.

This continued to happen with every supposedly wise man Socrates met. He questioned people about their beliefs, actions, and motives for their actions. As he continued to talk to a man, Socrates would subtly reveal the other's inconsistent beliefs. Like a hound dog, Socrates pursued the man's reasoning until the man became aware of the faults in his own thinking.

Socrates began by first questioning the political leaders. Then he questioned writers, poets, craftsmen, and any others who would speak with him. None of them had what Socrates considered to be wisdom. Socrates began to discover that those who believed they were the wisest were usually the most lacking.

Socrates' technique of interacting with others was by question and answer. The purpose was to discover how much a person knew and what he or she really believed. This method also forced people to examine those beliefs and decide whether or not those beliefs had a solid foundation.

As he practiced his technique, Socrates was also seeking answers to other questions—one of the main ones being the question of what makes a person good, wise, or happy. By applying the Socratic method, as his questioning came to be called, Socrates felt he was doing the god Apollo's work.

This mission of questioning the people of Athens now became Socrates' only occupation. His reputation as a wise man was growing. But he refused to call himself a teacher, and he would not accept money from those who wanted to learn from him. Socrates felt that he did not have enough knowledge or wisdom to ask for money. If he accepted payment, he reasoned, he would have to talk to anyone who paid him, whether he wanted to or not.

Barefoot and penniless, Socrates would make his way early every morning to the *agora*, or marketplace. Xenophon, one of Socrates' students, wrote, "When the agora became busy he was there in full view. He always spent the rest of the day where he could find the most company."

On rare occasions, in the evenings, Socrates would join in large parties called *symposia*, where men drank wine, played games, told stories, and debated ideas. He was good friends with many powerful Athenians. But he was willing to argue and talk

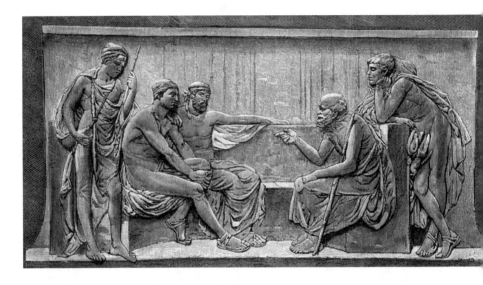

Socrates also talked to men at gyms where they exercised.

philosophy with nearly anyone—students and politicians, merchants and artists.

Socrates was perfectly fine with this lifestyle. But having so little may have been difficult for his wife, Xanthippe. They married in about 420 B.C., when Socrates was 49.

Socrates' lifestyle was not glamorous, and neither was his appearance. Many considered him physically ugly and said so. But wherever he went, he gathered a crowd of admirers around him.

Many of these were young men attracted to Socrates' extraordinary personality, and they were eager to learn from him. His followers admired the philosopher's self-confidence. They wanted to absorb his clever insights and acquire the same kind of deep, mysterious wisdom he seemed to have—as if he had

Socrates with his wife, Xanthippe, who was thought to be much younger than the philosopher

found the secret to life. They felt that simply being around Socrates made them better people.

Many Athenians, however, were not eager to endure Socrates or his methods. The questions that he raised were making him highly unpopular with the men he questioned and with some of the bystanders who listened in. Socrates would let no man rest if that man seemed smug or full of vanity about his own knowledge or status. Xenophon wrote, "Whenever they came into his company they had the annoyance of having their mistakes exposed."

Few wanted to be forced to look at whether they knew anything or whether the lives they were living were truly good and worthwhile. Many scorned Socrates for what they considered his annoying way of claiming to know nothing while proving he knew more than everyone he spoke to. Some said that Socrates' arguments were so strong that "men set upon him with their fists or tore their hair out."

Before long, Socrates was not only widely known for his wisdom

Plato and Xenophon together left the world the most complete writings about Socrates. Plato's Socrates is a brilliant philosopher and is subtle and insightful. But Xenophon's Socrates is a much more conventional character, more concerned with being self-disciplined and virtuous than with deep ideas. Was Socrates more like Plato's version, Xenophon's version, or a bit of both? Scholars around the world still argue about this question.

but he had also earned a reputation around Athens as a gadfly. His constant, irritating questioning was maddening, just like a horsefly that would not stop biting.

By his late 40s, Socrates had become famous enough around Athens to receive widespread public recognition. In 423, the Athenian playwright Aristophanes had produced a comedic play in which the main character was named Socrates. In this satire, called *Clouds*, Socrates is portrayed as an odd, unwashed schoolmaster who goes barefoot, gazes into the clouds, follows his own strange religion, and rolls his eyes at others' remarks.

Neither this play nor other expressions of anger toward him had much effect on Socrates' even-tempered, amused personality. He believed he had been appointed by the gods to wake his fellow Athenians up and remind them that pursuing wealth, fame, or power would not lead to happiness. The only lasting happiness came from perfecting the soul—living life as a deep, thoughtful, good human being.

For Socrates, the soul was the most important part of the individual. And once the soul achieved its highest good, no worldly concerns would matter. The soul would know the difference between right and wrong. Right action, Socrates said, must come from the soul's awareness of good and not be dictated by an ignorant society.

Socrates said that there was an ideal state of goodness. Once people recognized and understood this ideal, they would be incapable of acting wrongly. They would naturally begin to strive for excellence. And as they did so, their character and their lives would improve. Ultimately, they would be happier. It was conversation about serious issues that was most likely to persuade people to care for their souls.

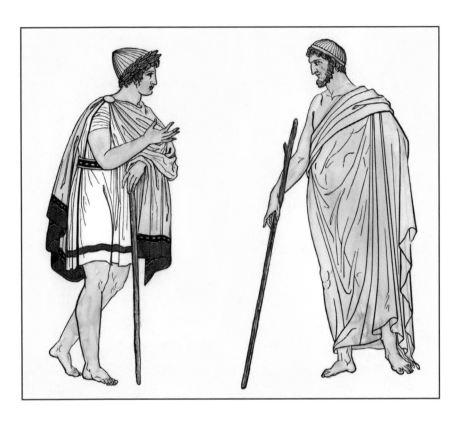

Citizens of Athens engaged in discussions throughout the city.

Socrates was convinced that no one would knowingly act wrongly. Those who did, he reasoned, simply did not yet understand what was truly right. This was why it was crucial, as the Oracle of Delphi proclaimed, to know oneself. Or, as Socrates expressed it, "The unexamined life isn't worth living for a human being." His divinely appointed job, as he understood it, was to help people examine their lives and become better people.

Because of the importance of examining one's beliefs and actions, Socrates strongly encouraged the young to think for themselves. He had observed that the so-called wise people of Athens had no idea what was truly wise or good or worth striving for. For that reason, it followed that the codes of behavior they devised for society would not always be in the best interest of the people.

Therefore, he advised the young to question everything they were taught rather than to just mindlessly conform. He warned them away from going along with society's accepted teachings and beliefs, especially since it was made up of so many unwise and foolish people.

In giving this advice, Socrates did not mean that people should feel free to ignore the laws and do whatever they wanted to do whenever they wanted. Rather, it was again a matter of first knowing what "right action" meant. In other words, they were to

Socrates and his followers

become philosophers and find true wisdom. This way, it would be impossible to do wrong.

This philosophy strongly appealed to the young people of Athens. Socrates' example of giving up worldly goals solely to seek wisdom, goodness, and truth inspired them to do likewise. They took up his style and began questioning for themselves, questioning everything—including their Athenian elders.

Socrates' influence over young men did not sit well with those who were against him, especially the fathers of some of these youths. It was not enough that Socrates badgered everyone in Athens. Now the young men were actually paying attention and raising their own questions. Socrates was beginning to express other troubling thoughts as well. Something had to be done about him. ℘

6 END OF A GOLDEN AGE

❧◊❧

Athens was in the midst of turbulence and drastic change. The city had not been directly attacked, but its military had been involved in a succession of sieges and battles since the start of the Peloponnesian War in 431 B.C. In the first 10 years of that war, Athens was defeated more than once while battling to keep her empire intact and gain dominance over Sparta.

After the deaths of Pericles in 429 and the Athenian leader Cleon in 423, the two city-states of Sparta and Athens, exhausted from war, signed another peace agreement in 421. That agreement, called the Peace of Nicias, was named after an Athenian general and negotiator. It stated that the two enemy city-states would stop fighting each other. Additionally, they agreed to defend each other for the next 50 years.

Alcibiades was one of Socrates' close friends.

During the Peace of Nicias, Socrates' young friend Alcibiades was elected to Athens' board of 10 generals. Socrates had saved the young Alcibiades' life at the Potidaean battle. Now, at 30, Alcibiades was considered one of Athens' most beautiful, brilliant, brave, and charismatic citizens. His own father had been an Athenian military commander, but when he was killed, Pericles had become Alcibiades' guardian.

Socrates had a particular love for Alcibiades because of his brilliant mind and the promise he showed. Alcibiades had once had an equally deep respect for Socrates. Now, however, Alcibiades' interests had turned to worldly things. By the time he was elected general, he had virtually abandoned the values he had learned from Socrates, though he still loved the man. As a grown man, Alcibiades was full of selfish ambition and desire for wealth, fame, and power—everything that Socrates scorned.

This ambition did not help Athens' peace

agreement with Sparta. The uneasy truce between the two city-states had begun to break down almost as soon as it was declared. Diplomatic relations again gave way to aggression. The now-powerful Alcibiades persuaded the Assembly of citizens—over the objections of his fellow general, Nicias—that an invasion of Sicily would provide food for the Athenians and tall trees to repair the fleet's masts. Nicias argued that the invasion would bring Sparta back into the war. Nicias was right. The 50-year Peace of Nicias had barely lasted six years when Alcibiades, Nicias, and Lamachus were appointed by the Assembly of citizens to lead the invasion.

In late 416, as the fleet was preparing to sail, almost all the city's sacred statues of Hermes, the god of travel, were mutilated in a single night. Many saw the destruction as a sign that a conspiracy was brewing against Athens' democracy. Hysteria broke out in the city, charges flew in all directions, and men were fleeing the city to avoid execution.

In that climate, Alcibiades was twice accused of sacrilege. Although he demanded a trial, he was outwitted by his enemies and set sail under a cloud of suspicion. When his enemies thought they had enough information to convict him, they sent for him. In early 415, en route to invade Sicily, Alcibiades jumped ship and escaped before being arrested. He fled to Sparta where his family had ties.

Nicias and Lamachus continued the Sicilian invasion, but they were not lucky. In Sparta, Alcibiades offered his help against Athens, which the Spartans enthusiastically accepted. By 413, aided by Alcibiades' excellent advice, Sicily had, with Spartan help, entirely wiped out or enslaved all the Athenians in Sicily. Later, when it was clear to everyone that he

During the Peloponnesian War, city-states supported either Athens or Sparta.

had been framed, the army insisted he return to lead them again, which he did successfully.

Socrates, now too old for hand-to-hand fighting in heavy armor, remained in Athens. He was well into middle age and had no desire to leave the city. He felt he had work to do as a gadfly and a seeker of truth. But the fortunes of the city were rapidly changing. So were people's attitudes toward Socrates. In his earlier years, he had been seen as more of a harmless annoyance than a danger. But with the destruction of the statues of Hermes and the humiliating defeat in Sicily, a dark mood had fallen across Athens. In this atmosphere of suspicion and fear, Socrates' influence over the young men of Athens suddenly took on ominous tones, making him increasingly unpopular.

Many Athenians considered Socrates' claims about the gods and his outspoken opinions about Athens' leading citizens a serious threat. Unlike most of his fellow citizens, Socrates saw democracy as hardly an ideal system of government, and he was not shy about probing its weaknesses.

One of Socrates' main objections was the way in which political positions were filled. In Athens, people were chosen for all political jobs except military general by lot—names were randomly selected from among those on the tribal lists of citizens. But they had no training whatsoever for such jobs.

Socrates considered this particular democratic

practice pure idiocy. It was the luck of the draw, he pointed out, that placed many entirely untrained, uneducated, and inexperienced citizens in service as judges and in other important civic jobs. How good could that be for the city? No one would employ an unqualified person to serve as a carpenter, a musician, or in any other job, Socrates reasoned, just because his name had been drawn. Therefore, why do so for the most important positions of authority that existed?

The freedom-loving Athenians feared Socrates was infecting their sons with these rebellious ideas. In 414 B.C., the playwright Aristophanes wrote lines that indicated the attitudes of the average Athenian citizens. In his comedy *The Birds*, he refers to a group of young, dirty, stick-wielding, pro-Sparta Athenians as being "Socratified."

But the youth were not the only Socratified Athenians. As a result of the unsuccessful war against Sparta in Sicily, many of Athens' wealthy citizens had suffered financial loss. Some cities formerly loyal to Athens had revolted, shrinking the size of the once-powerful Athenian Empire. Scores of Athenians were fed up with the citizen Assembly that had followed Alcibiades into an unwinnable war, especially those who were intellectuals and aristocrats.

By 411, Athens was ripe for revolution. Athens' constitution was abolished, and oligarchs, or a group of powerful men, took power, led by Athenian aristocrats. This so-called Council of 400 lasted only four months. Democracy was swiftly restored with the help of Alcibiades. The army, knowing him to be a brilliant strategist and a man others would follow, recalled him to lead them. Alcibiades now returned to command what remained of Athens' military. Under him, the Athenian navy defeated Sparta in battles at sea. After the 400 were pushed out, a larger council of 5,000 antidemocratic Athenians was established, but the city's democrats took control again almost immediately.

In Greek comedies like The Birds, *actors wore masks.*

War, political upheaval, and the struggle for power became ever more intense. Athens' citizen Assembly foolishly refused to establish peace with Sparta, and the Peloponnesian War raged on for the next three years with no decisive victor. In 406, when Socrates was 63 years old, Athens scored a victory at sea against Sparta in the Battle of Arginusae. After the battle, a storm came up, and the captains who had been ordered to recover many dead and wounded soldiers were unable to do so.

This outraged the Athenians, who felt it was especially important to bury the corpses. Although the whole board of 10 generals was originally charged with what seemed to the Assembly to be a crime, only six returned to Athens to face the court. But the

The Peloponnesian War lasted 27 years, from 431 to 404 B.C. and ended in victory for Sparta.

way in which the court handled the trial was illegal by Athenian law.

As it turned out, on the day the generals were brought to trial, Socrates' tribe was in charge of presiding over the council. This group of 50 men had been selected for duty by lot. By law, each general was supposed to have his own separate trial, but all were being tried together. Within the presiding committee, only a few objected to these illegal proceedings. One was Socrates.

The objections that Socrates and the few others raised enraged the majority. These men declared that anyone who objected would share the same fate as the generals. At this, almost all of those who had disagreed backed down—but not Socrates. He fearlessly maintained his position.

Now the Assembly turned on Socrates. They shouted insults and threatened him with arrest. Still, he stood his ground. Perhaps shamed by Socrates' moral stand, the Assembly agreed to vote on whether the generals should receive separate trials. Some voted with Socrates to give each general his own trial. But opponents maneuvered the proceedings, making sure the generals would be tried together. The Assembly then decided to execute the generals. For a citizen Assembly, moved by emotional speeches, to execute its remaining military leaders in wartime was a perfect example of what could go wrong in a democracy when the Assembly could disregard the laws. Socrates said:

> *I thought I should face danger on the side of law and justice, rather than go along with you for fear of imprisonment or death when your proposals were unjust.*

He did what he believed was right, even though he risked imprisonment or execution himself.

During the next year, 405 B.C., Athens suffered the disastrous consequences of its hasty actions. In a battle that led to the city's downfall, Sparta destroyed nearly the entire Athenian navy, the backbone of Athens' defense. Alcibiades had offered the Athenians good advice beforehand, but they had ignored him. It was a final fatal decision.

In the spring of 404, the Spartans laid siege to the city and took complete control of Athens. The Athenians were forced to surrender, and the long defense walls protecting the city were torn down.

Worse, the citizen Assembly elected 30 men to rewrite the constitution, bringing back the predemocratic one. Those men, known as The Thirty, quickly abandoned writing a constitution, choosing instead to rule Athens themselves. One of the leaders of this repressive and bloody regime was a man named Critias, the wealthy second cousin of Socrates' bright young companion Plato. Critias

Spartans destroyed the walls of Athens in 404 B.C.

had also been a companion of Socrates briefly. Comparing Critias and Alcibiades, Xenophon wrote:

> *These two men were by nature the most ambitious persons in all Athens. ... As soon as they felt superior to the rest of the company they broke away from Socrates and took up politics, the object for which they had courted his society.*

The Thirty took charge with brutal measures, wiping out many freedoms the Athenians had formerly enjoyed. They seized land and other property. They executed 1,500 citizens and foreign residents, targeting wealthy, prominent democrats and anyone who spoke out against The Thirty. Thousands of

Athenians fled into exile. Even moderate oligarchs feared for their lives.

The Thirty wrote new citizenship rules. The result was that out of more than 20,000 Athenian citizens, under the oligarchy, only 3,000 qualified to make decisions. The others had all their weapons confiscated. Supporters of democracy who had been living outside of the city walls were assassinated. Exiled democrats, including Socrates' childhood friend Chaerephon, gathered to plot the overthrow of The Thirty.

Throughout these dark days, Socrates remained in Athens. But he did not go unnoticed. Hoping to give him a part in their deadly game, The Thirty ordered Socrates to help with the capture of a democratic general whom they planned to execute. Socrates refused. Plato recorded him as saying:

> *They gave many such orders to many other people too, of course, since they wanted to implicate as many as possible in their crimes. On that occasion, however, I showed once again not by words but by deeds that I couldn't care less about death—if that isn't putting it too bluntly—but that all I care about is not doing anything unjust or impious.*

No one knows whether Socrates would have been executed for this disobedience. Before the oligarchs had a chance to deal with him, the democrats landed at the Piraeus harbor, and fighting broke out there. The Thirty went to the harbor to fight, where the vicious Critias was killed. Those of The Thirty who survived began leaving the city within months. Many of the oligarchs left Athens for the *deme*, or political district within Attica, of Eleusis, where they had killed all the citizens.

Within a matter of about eight months, democracy was restored in Athens. But the democrats did not trust the oligarchs who had retreated. Despite an amnesty negotiated by the Spartans, at their first opportunity, the democrats rushed to Eleusis and wiped out the oligarchs, saying they had been hiring mercenaries to plot a comeback.

Socrates refused to cooperate with The Thirty.

The Peloponnesian War had finally come to an end after 27 years of intermittent battle. It was also the end of Athens' Golden Age. Athens would never regain the power it had once had. But the government of the people had been fully restored. ❧

7 CRIMINAL CHARGES

ᑫᕙᔆᕗ

One of those who had hidden away in the mountains during the oligarchic rampage was a wealthy leader in the democracy named Anytus. He had at first sided with The Thirty, then he helped lead the counterrevolution that drove them out and brought democracy back to Athens. By the spring of 399 B.C., Anytus was a powerful politician. And he had grievances against Socrates. So did others.

Socrates had swayed the minds of young men and, with his frequent questions, had publicly and arrogantly made many of the city's most respected elders look like fools. And wasn't he against the gods worshipped by the rest of the Hellenic society? He didn't even believe in them, Socrates' enemies declared. He followed his own deity, they said, which spoke to him in his head.

Around Athens, many people were in agreement about Socrates. He was a danger to the democracy. He was a corrupter of youth. And he was a mocker of the established state religion. All these things, they believed, proved one point: Socrates needed to be dealt with, one way or another. Xenophon quoted Socrates as saying, "Most people when they are set upon looking into other people's affairs never turn to examine themselves."

In the spring of 399 B.C., Anytus and the orator Lycon joined Meletus in filing criminal charges against Socrates. Meletus, the youngest of the three and the chief prosecutor, was a poet. Some also suspected him of being a religious fanatic.

Any citizen could begin court proceedings against another. But the charge had to be announced to the defendant before witnesses. This was the first step. The charges Meletus, Anytus, and Lycon brought against Socrates were twofold. The first allegation was the charge of impiety, or "not acknowledging the gods the city acknowledges, but new daimonic activities instead." This was the charge that fired Meletus' negative energies. Socrates had publicly stated his opinion that the gods necessarily must be all good, incapable of wrong action. But the Greeks knew their gods to be greedy, selfish, and jealous. They lied, stole, and murdered. So how could he believe in the

gods that the Athenians worshipped? This attitude outraged the rigid-thinking, traditional believers.

Many other Athenians also ridiculed traditional religious beliefs. But Socrates had an additional

Athenians were required to show their devotion to the Greek gods by making sacrificial offerings and participating in many other long-established religious rites and festivals. People like Socrates, who had unconventional religious views and did not believe the stories of the evil words and deeds of the Olympian gods, were seen as a danger to society. If such people were not controlled or stopped, the Athenians believed, the city would suffer punishment. Athena, Zeus, or Apollo might bring disaster down on them at any moment.

strike against him—his daimon. Added to this, some suspected that Meletus was angered by negative comments that Socrates had made against revered Greek poetry.

The second allegation was that of corrupting Athens' youth. Some have speculated that Anytus was most motivated by this particular charge because his own son had been influenced by Socrates' views. According to Socrates' admirer Xenophon, Socrates had advised Anytus' son against taking on the work his father had arranged for him—the "slavish way of life" of a tanner. But Plato, who shows Socrates praising Anytus' father highly as a self-made man, contradicts this.

With the public announcement of these charges, Meletus informed Socrates that he had four days to appear at the Royal Stoa, the place where the laws of Athens were displayed. There the charges against Socrates would be officially filed. If he did not appear, the lawsuit would go ahead unchallenged. At this point, Socrates had the legal option of voluntarily

choosing exile and leaving the city at once.

Socrates chose to remain in Athens and meet the charges. He appeared with Meletus at the Royal Stoa. There the magistrate in charge, called the king archon and chosen by lot, determined that Athenian law would allow the lawsuit. An announcement of

Socrates made the fatal decision to remain in Athens and face the charges against him.

The king archon to whom Meletus brought his charges had authority to choose from among three actions. He could have sent the case on to a lesser legal body that would act as a mediator between the accusers and the accused. He could have entirely dismissed the case. Or he could accept the case and send it on to a formal trial—which is what the king archon chose to do. The original document that detailed the charges against Socrates survived for at least 500 years in a public archive, where it was copied. The original is now lost, however, like almost everything else that was written in ancient times.

the charges, written on whitened tablets, was posted publicly in the Royal Stoa, and a preliminary hearing was scheduled.

The news of these charges and the upcoming hearing swept through Athens, creating a fury of mixed reactions, gossip, and speculation about what would happen next. But in spite of the question about his fate and the uproar around him, Socrates remained as calm and cheerful as always. This did not surprise his friends and supporters.

Xenophon wrote that after Meletus had entered the charges, a friend named Hermogenes came across Socrates discussing philosophy as usual. Startled, Hermogenes asked Socrates why he was not hard at work preparing his defense.

Socrates replied, "Don't you see that I have been preparing for it all my life?" When Hermogenes asked how this was true, Socrates pointed out that he had spent his entire life focusing only on the question of right and wrong, which he considered the best possible way to prepare for a defense. Finally, he added that at first he had been thinking about how he should defend himself to the jury, but his daimon had stopped him. "I have already set about considering my defence before the jury, and my divine sign opposed it."

The purpose of the preliminary hearing was to clarify the issues of the case. After the king archon questioned both Socrates and Meletus, they had an opportunity to question each other. At the end of these proceedings, the king archon agreed that the case had merit. Only a month or two later, Socrates would go to trial. ✣

8 THE TRIAL OF THE CENTURY

Chapter

❧⁓⊱⊰⁓❧

Socrates had used the so-called Socratic method of questioning to expose people's vanity and egotism throughout Athens. This had delighted his friends and disciples. But it had enraged his enemies.

One of the most important documents that has survived from this time is *The Apology*, written by Plato. It is a dramatic account of Socrates' argument in his own defense at the trial. But Socrates was not the first to speak. In accordance with court law, Meletus had the floor first, representing the prosecution. The time would be carefully measured by a water clock, and each side was given the same amount of time for presenting its case, including the calling of witnesses.

The water clock, an ancient timing device, was

simply a large urn filled with water that had a small hole drilled in its bottom. Once the pot had drained completely, drop by drop, the speaker's time was up. Another citizen, also chosen by lot, watched over the water clock as the trial proceeded.

The prosecutors detailed Socrates' religious offenses and the charges of corruption against him. As the water clock drained, they reminded the jury that the defendant would use his clever arguments to try to mislead and confuse them.

When the accusers had finished speaking, all eyes turned to Socrates. It was his turn. Beginning humbly, he assured the jury that he would speak in his own simple style and tell only the truth. But then he got to work. Immediately, Socrates launched into discussing the old prejudices against him and how

An ancient Greek water clock was used in court to time speeches.

they came to be. He reminded his listeners of the negative—and false—ways he had been portrayed by the city's playwrights. He strenuously denied that he was anyone's teacher and reminded the jurors that he lived in poverty and never took fees.

Many in attendance were much younger than Socrates and probably had not heard about the Oracle of Delphi's answer to Chaerephon's question years earlier. Now he recounted this story again, to explain why he had spent his life always talking and arguing. He admitted that this activity was the source of his bad reputation as a gadfly. But this diligent search for truth had gotten him only poverty, scorn, a following of wealthy young imitators, and charges that he was corrupting these youths.

> *The young people who follow me around of their own accord, those who have the most leisure, the sons of the very rich, enjoy listening to people being cross-examined. They often imitate me themselves and in turn attempt to cross-examine others. ... The result is that those they question are angry not at themselves, but at me.*

Three separate times, Socrates addressed the issue of corrupting the young. He stated that if he had done so, it had not been on purpose. Therefore, he reasoned, he should be taught how to avoid this fault rather than be tried for a crime. Many perhaps were on his side at this point.

As usual, Socrates sounded reasonable as he continued with his case. He pointed out his heroic service in battle. Forging ahead, he effortlessly out-argued Meletus. Soon the Socratic method had exposed the confused and illogical basis of the prosecution's argument. By the end of the cross-examination, a deeply befuddled Meletus was forced to admit that the charges concerning religion were faulty as well.

By mocking and belittling Meletus, however, Socrates seemed to be taking a reckless path. As if wanting to make matters worse, he then made another bold declaration. He would never give up philosophy, the work Apollo had given him to do—even though the Athenians might command him to stop. Rather than corrupting anyone, he informed them, the questions he raised had only improved the people, whether they realized it or not. He said:

> *I've literally been attached to the city, as if to a large thoroughbred horse that was somewhat sluggish because of its size and needed to be awakened by some sort of gadfly. It's as just such a gadfly, it seems to me, that the god has attached me to the city—one that awakens, cajoles, and reproaches each and every one of you and never stops alighting everywhere on you the whole day.*

These and many other things that Socrates said were not the kinds of things the jury or others in the court were happy to hear. He might have humbled himself and begged for mercy. These were the tactics that other Athenian defendants normally used to get sympathy and lesser sentences. Instead, as always, Socrates remained true to who he was and what he believed in. He spoke the truths that he saw.

But now, his few hours for defending himself were nearly over. Socrates' long, fearless, and defiant defense had been anything but apologetic. As if boldly challenging the jury, he proclaimed, "I wouldn't act in any other way, not even if I were to die many times over."

By a vote of 281-220, Socrates was found guilty. Now, taking on the role of judge, the jury's next task was to decide the punishment as well.

In this phase of the trial, the law required both

Athens' jury members, chosen by lot, were known as the dikastai. Besides being at least 30 years old and a citizen, each selected juror had to take a dikastic oath at the beginning of the year to qualify to serve on various juries all year. Every day, a new configuration of jurors was selected, and often these juries had more than 500 members. Large numbers helped prevent people from trying to bribe jurors, as did the fact that trials could last only a day, leaving no time to contact jurors in their homes to bribe them. An uneven number of dikastai ensured that there would not be a tie when it came to voting on conviction and punishment.

the defendant and the prosecutor to suggest a punishment. The prosecutors wasted no time asking that Socrates be put to death. But Socrates continued on his infuriating path. Outrageously, he first suggested that he receive, at the public's expense, free meals for life in the town hall, the place where Olympic Games winners were honored. "Nothing could be more appropriate," Socrates told the jury. This did not go over well, and Socrates was asked to come up with some other punishment. His reply was that he did not think he deserved a penalty of any kind because he had never done anything wrong on purpose.

Pressed, he suggested a fine of a single *mina*, or a few dollars. This was a further insult that put the jury into an uproar. Finally, Socrates offered to pay 30 minas, an amount that equaled about six times what his meager fortune was worth and was equal to a few hundred dollars today. He reluctantly agreed to this only after his friends in the audience, including Plato, insisted and offered to pay the sum on his behalf.

The trial had by now gone on for several hours. Perhaps because they were angered and fed up with Socrates' apparent arrogance and lack of remorse—or perhaps because they thought the city should not tempt the gods by sparing the life of a man convicted of impiety—when they cast their final votes, many more were now against Socrates. By a count of 361-140, Socrates was condemned to death.

Upon hearing this verdict, the unrepentant gadfly rose calmly and gave a final, eloquent speech. In the same truth-telling style he used in the agora, Socrates fearlessly accepted his fate and spoke his final words to the court :

> *But now it's time to leave, I to die and you to live. Which of us goes to the better thing, however, is unclear to everyone except the god.* 🙰

After the jury voted to execute Socrates, he made a prediction. He told the court that if they put him to death, they would soon become the objects of hatred themselves. Socrates reasoned that those who were against the jury's decision would claim that Socrates was wise, even though he never claimed that himself. According to the ancient moralizer Diogenes Laertius, whose stories one must take with a grain of salt, this prediction did come true. The Athenians drove Anytus and Lycon out of the city and won a death sentence against Meletus. Anytus fled to the city of Heraclea, but before a single day had passed, the citizens there banished him, too.

9 Swan Song

✦

Socrates was sleeping peacefully and dreaming. As dawn broke, he awoke to find his old friend Crito waiting in the prison cell with him. Crito had been to visit Socrates many times since he had been imprisoned. This time, he tipped the jailer when he entered, because he was on an important mission.

"I bring bad news," Crito told Socrates, according to Plato's famous dramatic work also called *Crito*. "Not bad in your view, it seems to me, but bad and hard in mine and that of all your friends—and hardest of all, I think, for me to bear."

At once, Socrates guessed what the trouble was. A ship was about to arrive in Athens. On the day before Socrates' trial, that ship had set sail from Athens to the island of Delos. The trip by sea was an important

The sacred voyage to Delos commemorated the Greek hero Theseus, who had sailed to Crete and killed the mythical Minotaur, a deadly beast that was half bull and half man. By doing so, Theseus had released Athens from its annual payment to King Minos of seven girls and seven boys. Before sailing, the ship was loaded with offerings to the god Apollo, who the Hellenes believed was born on Delos. By sending a ship full of offerings to the god, the Athenians hoped to receive blessings and protection from him.

religious ritual that occurred every year. While the ship was away, the people of Athens performed ritual purification rites, and all executions were postponed.

Ordinarily, Socrates would have been executed within 24 hours of his trial. But with the sacred ship gone, he was spared. Rather than facing immediate death, he had sat in prison for about 30 days. Now Crito was bringing news that the ship was approaching Athens on its return voyage and was expected that very day. Once it returned, business, including death, would go on as usual. Executions would be scheduled for the following day.

As always, Socrates was serene, even in the face of this news. He had just awakened from a dream that was still with him. In that dream, a beautiful woman dressed in white robes had told him, "Socrates, you will arrive in fertile Phthia on the third day." Phthia was the home of the Greeks' great hero Achilles, and to Socrates, the meaning of his dream was clear. His soul would go on to the afterlife on the third day after his dream, which meant that the ship would not arrive that day but the following day.

Now Crito launched into the reason he had come. He was going to help Socrates escape, not only from prison but from Athens itself. Crito and many other friends of Socrates had it all planned out.

But Socrates gently refused his old friend. He was ready to meet his fate. He would face death with no fear or resistance.

Crito pleaded and begged. He put forth his most persuasive arguments, trying to coax Socrates to change his mind and save himself from death. "After all, we're surely justified in running this risk to save you or an even greater one if need be." But Socrates knew that he could not stay in Athens if he escaped and that he would never be happy if he went into exile in some other city. He had never left Athens at all, except for military service.

Also, he pointed out to Crito, now that he had accepted his sentence, he would be breaking the law if he escaped. And since breaking the law would be wrong, he could not possibly do anything but accept his fate. If he did otherwise, he argued, everyone could say he was just as bad as those he constantly challenged. Even in the face of death, Socrates was using his brilliant Socratic method to make Crito see his point. Socrates replied:

No, as far as my present thoughts go, at least, you may be sure that if you argue against them, you will speak in vain. All the same, if you think you can do any more, please tell me.

Frustrated and resigned that he would be unable to convince his dear friend, Crito gave up. "No, Socrates, I've nothing to say," he replied.

Ironically, if in court Socrates had suggested exile as his punishment, most historians believe that the majority would have gone along with that sentence. Many think his prosecutors did not really want Socrates' death. They just wanted him silenced or out of Athens. Even if he had escaped from prison and left the city, it is unlikely that anyone would have hunted him and dragged him back. But if Socrates had chosen any path other than death, he would have been going against everything he believed and had tried to show others his entire life. He had no desire even to attempt escape.

On his fateful last day, The Eleven—the officials in charge of the prison—came to Socrates at dawn. They unlocked Socrates from his chains and informed him that the ship had docked the day before. They confirmed that he would be executed that day and told him what to expect.

Throughout Socrates' month of imprisonment, his friends had come to talk with him in his cell every day. On this morning, they arrived as early as possible. Most of what is known about Socrates' final day is told in Plato's famous work *Phaedo*. In that dramatic dialogue, Phaedo, a former slave and young companion of Socrates, travels to a remote village in northwestern Peloponnesus after Socrates' death. There he relates the details of the sad event to a friend named Echecrates and others in the community. Plato was apparently not present at Socrates' death, probably because he was ill. But Phaedo's experience of the death scene comes across powerfully.

When they got to Socrates' cell, Phaedo tells Echecrates, they found Xanthippe already there. She was sitting beside her husband, their youngest child in her lap. Shortly, Socrates suggested gently that she should be taken home. Crito's servants came to

Plato's Phaedo *was written around 360 B.C., and portions of a later ancient copy of it still exist today.*

escort her, and Xanthippe left Socrates, weeping.

Socrates had one last day to converse with his friends and followers. Gathered there with him were at least 15 men, young and old. All of them valued the life of the mind more than the body and were full of sorrow to think that they would no longer have the pleasure of his company. But Socrates himself was in an excellent mood, even happy.

He remained that way throughout the day, as eager for lively argument as ever. As the hours ticked away, Socrates led those gathered with him through an inspection of many topics. The men argued over the existence and nature of the soul. They also discussed the afterlife—if there was one and what it would be like. Socrates expressed his enthusiasm

Even while in prison, Socrates continued to challenge the beliefs of his companions.

for having an opportunity to philosophize with all the great souls who would be waiting in the underworld.

He told his friends that he would be glad to be released from the burden of the mortal body and vigorously defended his belief in the immortality of the soul. He envisioned philosophers being admitted to a better world after death than the lower one reserved for those who only pursued worldly goals.

As the day wore on, the mood, Phaedo says, went from light to dark and back again. Laughter turned into tears, and tears to laughter. Phaedo told Echecrates:

> *Though I have admired Socrates on many occasions, I have never found him more wonderful than at that moment. That he should not be at a loss for a reply is perhaps not surprising; but what I especially admired was, first, the pleasure, the kindness, the respect with which he received those young men's observations, and secondly ... the success with which he healed our distress.*

Finally, a long silence set in. Then one of Socrates' friends commented that he didn't want to say anything to upset Socrates in his time of misfortune. Socrates laughed kindly and replied, "It looks as if I should have a hard job to convince the world in general that I don't consider my present situation a sad one, when I can't convince even you two."

Socrates then compared himself to the swan, a bird sacred to Apollo:

> *For they, when they realize that they have to die, sing more and sing more sweetly than they have ever sung before, rejoicing at the prospect of going into the presence of that god whose servants they are ... human beings, because of their own fear of death, malign them, making out that their departing song is a painful lament for death; they fail to reflect that no bird sings when it is hungry or cold or feels any sort of pain, not even the nightingale itself ... what I think is that belonging as they do to Apollo, they are prophetic creatures who foresee the blessings in store for them in Hades, and therefore sing with greater delight on that last day than ever before.*

All who were listening saw how Socrates was like the swan he described, a faithful servant of Apollo. And now he displayed a peaceful joyousness in the face of death. Socrates' companions understood, even if they did not all believe in the soul or an afterlife, that he was comparing himself with the swan to reassure them that all was well.

The day had been filled with philosophy. Now evening was approaching. It was time to address practical matters. Overcoming his grief, Crito asked

Socrates for any last instructions. He wanted to know if Socrates had any requests regarding his family and what his friends could do to please Socrates most.

"Just the things I'm always saying, Crito ... nothing very new," Socrates replied. "If you take care of your own selves, you'll please both me and mine and yourselves in whatever you do."

"But how are we to bury you?" Crito wanted to know.

Socrates laughed gently. "Whatever way you like ... provided you can catch me, and I don't elude you." Then he told Crito to do whatever was usually done

Socrates calmed his friends before his own execution.

or whatever he thought best.

Socrates was just reminding Crito and the rest of his friends that the physical body mattered little to him. He had no concern over what would happen to his corpse, whether it was buried or burned. His life and being were in his soul, and that soul might well be bound for blessings. "When I drink the poison," he said, "I'll … take my leave of you and depart for certain happy conditions of the blessed."

Socrates said other things to comfort Crito and the others, and then rose to go to the bath chamber. By religious custom, it would have been up to Xanthippe and the other women of his household to wash

Socrates' corpse. By bathing at the prison, he was sparing them this task. After he was finished bathing, he called for his children. The women of the house came again, bringing his three sons—a nearly 17-year-old, a small boy, and a toddler. Socrates talked with his children, giving them some final instructions while Crito sat by. Then his family left for good. Socrates returned to his gathered friends.

It was nearly sunset. The men had little to say now, and the mood was somber. Soon the jailer, a public slave appointed by The Eleven, arrived. Speaking emotionally, the jailer told Socrates that other prisoners cursed him and always became angry at him at the time of their death, even though the jailer was only obeying orders in making them drink the poison. He called Socrates "the most decent, gentlest, and best man who's ever come to this place." He said he knew Socrates would not be angry with him. "Fare you well, and try to bear the inevitable as easily as you can," he finished. With these words, the man burst into tears and turned to leave.

Socrates returned the jailer's good wishes and said he would drink the poison without feeling angry. To his friends, he had only kind words for the man.

"And now how decent of him to weep for me! Come then, Crito, let's do as he asks and have the poison brought if it's ready."

At this, Crito and the others protested strenuously.

The setting rays of the sun were still shining across the hills, Crito pointed out. There was still plenty of time. Those condemned often had dinner and stayed with their friends late into the night before taking the poison. The men begged Socrates to do the same.

"It's quite reasonable, Crito, for those people to do those things since they think they gain something by doing them," Socrates responded.

At this, Socrates insisted that the deadly hemlock drink be brought to him. Crito nodded to a slave who was standing there with them, and the slave went out. After a long while, he returned with the man, another public slave, whose job it was to give the poison. In the man's hand was the cup of death.

Socrates asked for instructions. The man told him that after he drank the hemlock, he should walk around until his legs felt heavy. Then he should lie down, and the poison would do its work. Saying this, he handed the cup to Socrates. Before taking the drink, Socrates gave a quick prayer to the gods, asking that his journey from the physical world to their realm be fortunate for him. Then, as his friends looked on, Socrates calmly downed the poison in one swallow. Now the men's sorrow could not be contained. Phaedo said:

In my own case, the tears were pouring
down my cheeks despite my efforts, so that

I covered my face and wept for myself—not for him, certainly not, but for my own misfortune in losing such a man as a friend. Crito had got up and moved away even before I did, when he was unable to hold back his tears. And Apollodorus, who earlier still had been weeping steadily, now burst forth in such a storm of tears and distress that he made everyone present break down—except, that is, for Socrates himself.

Socrates was the only one who remained completely calm.

What a way to behave, my friends! ... Why it was for just this reason, you know, that I sent the women away, so they wouldn't commit these sorts of errors. I've heard indeed that one should die in reverent silence. Come, mind your behavior and control yourselves.

In Greece, few people were imprisoned during Socrates' time or in the following several centuries. Offenders were punished by paying fines, being exiled from their city-state, or by immediate death. Prisoners of war were held for ransom. Hemlock was the standard method of execution. After death, the body would be bathed in water from a well in the prison. Then it would be wrapped in a shroud and either burned or buried as the family wished. Women also had the important task of formal mourning. They would publicly display grief by wailing, pulling out their hair, and tearing at their faces.

Socrates' words made his friends feel ashamed, and they quieted. When the poison had coursed halfway up his body, he spoke his last words: "Crito, we owe a cock to Asclepius.

Please, don't forget to pay the debt." Asclepius was the Greek god of medicine and healing. By sacrificing a rooster, Socrates was saying, perhaps, that he had been cured of the worldly burdens he had to bear. The poison then claimed him.

Socrates died in 399 B.C., but he lived on in the minds and hearts of his friends, who, during his life, gathered around him because of the great value they felt from being in his company. He helped them be more insightful, more tolerant, more perceptive, and more thoughtful about the world around them.

Socrates' companions were sickened by his death. They gave up trying to get the people of Athens to understand what their teacher had been trying to show them. Many of his companions, including Plato, left Athens and went into exile.

Socrates' life has been reconstructed mainly through the works of Plato and Xenophon. These and the other surviving fragments have given historians and philosophers a lot to think about. Today, the debate about how much of the real Socrates exists in these works is known as the Socratic Problem. The wise man that Plato and Xenophon have shown the world is like a jewel with many facets. There are always new angles from which to look at Socrates.

Of the two writers, Xenophon and Plato, Xenophon was by far the more simple and less poetic or philosophical. But sometimes his plain style can

provide the last word. In the final paragraph of his work *Memoirs of Socrates*, Xenophon wrote about his teacher:

A statue of Socrates stands outside the Hellenic Academy in Athens, Greece.

> *He seemed to me to be the perfect example of goodness and happiness. If anyone disapproves of this assessment, let him compare other people's characters with [Socrates'] qualities, and then make his own decision.* ও

SOCRATES' LIFE

451 B.C.

Begins two years of mandatory military training

469 B.C.

Born in Athens, Greece

470 B.C.

468 B.C.

Sophocles wins first tragedy drama prize

456 B.C.

A gold and ivory statue of Zeus, one of the seven wonders of the ancient world, is built in Olympia

WORLD EVENTS

450 B.C.

Meets and has dialogue with great visiting philosophers

439 B.C.

Turns 30 and becomes eligible for additional offices under the democratic lottery system

450 B.C.

441 B.C.

Sophocles produces *Antigone* in Athens

450 B.C.

The first bank is founded in Athens

SOCRATES' LIFE

425 B.C.

Serves as a hoplite in
the Battle of Delium

429 B.C.

Serves as a hoplite
in battle and siege of
Potidaea, and saves
the life of Alcibiades

425 B.C.

432 B.C.

The Parthenon in
Athens is completed

424 B.C.

The great philosopher
Plato is born

WORLD EVENTS

423 B.C.

Is mocked in
Aristophanes'
comedy *Clouds;*
serves as a hoplite
in the battle of
Amphipolis

420 B.C.

Marries Xanthippe;
they would have three
sons

420 B.C.

421 B.C.

Peace of Nicias brings
temporary end to the
Peloponnesian War
between Athens
and Sparta

420 B.C.

Protagoras, a Greek
philosopher who
coined the phrase
"Man is the measure
of all things," dies; a
crater on the moon is
named after him

406 B.C.

Protests illegal prose-
cution of generals after
Battle of Arginusae

414 B.C. In his
play *The Birds*,
Aristophanes calls
pro-Spartan youth
"Socratified"

415 B.C.

413 B.C.

Athens is defeated
by Syracuse and loses
its entire fleet

415 B.C.

First performance
of Euripides'
Trojan Women

399 B.C.

Criminal charges brought against him; convicted at trial and sentenced to death; dies after drinking poison

404 B.C.

Attacked by Aristophanes again in his comedy *Frogs*

404 B.C.

Athens surrenders to Sparta; Thirty Tyrants rule Athens, executing at least 1,500 people as 5,000 people flee or are exiled

399 B.C.

Plato and others begin to write about Socrates

DATE OF BIRTH: 469 B.C.

BIRTHPLACE: Alopece district of
ancient Athens

FATHER: Sophroniscus

MOTHER: Phaenarete

SPOUSE: Xanthippe

DATE OF MARRIAGE: About 420 B.C.

CHILDREN: Lamprocles
Sophroniscus
Menexenus

DATE OF DEATH: 399 B.C.

Further Reading

Bordessa, Kris. *Tools of the Ancient Greeks: A Kid's Guide to the History & Science of Life in Ancient Greece.* White River Junction, Vt.: Nomad Press, 2006.

Roberts, Jennifer T., and Tracy Barrett. *The Ancient Greek World.* New York: Oxford University Press, 2004.

Weate, Jeremy. *A Young Person's Guide to Philosophy: "I Think, Therefore I am."* New York: DK Publishing, 1998.

White, David A. *Philosophy for Kids: 40 Fun Questions That Help You Wonder ... About Everything!* Waco, Texas: Prufrock Press, 2000.

Zannos, Susan. *The Life and Times of Socrates.* Hockessin, Del.: Mitchell Lane Publishers, 2004.

Look for more Signature Lives books about this era:

Alexander the Great: *World Conqueror*
ISBN 0-7565-1872-5

Aristotle: *Philosopher, Teacher, and Scientist*
ISBN 0-7565-1873-3

Thucydides: *Ancient Greek Historian*
ISBN 0-7565-1875-X

On the Web

For more information on *Socrates*, use FactHound.

1. Go to *www.facthound.com*
2. Type in this book ID: 0756518741
3. Click on the *Fetch It* button.

FactHound will find the best Web sites for you.

Historic Sites

National Archaeological
Museum of Athens
44 Patission St.
106 82 Athens
Attica, Greece
011-30-210-8217724
Ancient Greek art including
sculpture, pottery, and bronzes

The Metropolitan Museum of Art
1000 Fifth Ave.
New York, NY 10028
212/535-7710
Artifacts, statues, and literature from
ancient Greece

amnesty
the act of an authority or government by which pardon is granted to a large group of individuals

B.C.
a Christian term meaning "before Christ" and referring to dates that occurred before the birth of Jesus; B.C. dates decrease as time goes on

deities
gods or goddesses

gadfly
a person who stimulates or annoys, especially by persistent criticism

impiety
a lack of proper respect for or failing in one's duties toward the gods

oligarchs
a few people who have power to rule all others

oracle
a priest or priestess who claimed to be able to speak to the gods

piety
a strong respect for deity and devotion to divine worship

sacrilege
gross irreverence to a sacred person, place, or thing

satire
literature that makes fun of human habits and failures

Chapter 1

Page 11, line 6: C.D.C. Reeve, ed. and trans. *The Trials of Socrates: Six Classic Texts by Plato, Aristophanes, and Xenophon.* Indianapolis: Hackett Pub. Co., 2002, pp. 26–27.

Page 11, line 15: Ibid., pp. 52–53.

Page 11, line 28: Ibid., p. 57.

Chapter 4

Page 32, line 1: Ibid., p. 47.

Chapter 5

Page 39, line 7: Ibid., pp. 32–33.

Page 41, line 3: Ibid., p. 33.

Page 42, line 21: Xenophon. *Memoirs of Socrates and the Symposium (The Dinner Party)* (trans. Hugh Tredennick). Harmondsworth, UK.: Penguin Books, 1970, p. 8.

Page 45, line 3: Ibid., p. 47.

Page 45, line 17: "Socrates." *The Lives of Eminent Philosophers.* Diogenes Laertius. 3 Feb. 2006.

www.law.umkc.edu/faculty/projects/ftrials/socrates/socratesbio.html

Page 47, line 6: *The Trials of Socrates: Six Classic Texts by Plato, Aristophanes, and Xenophon,* p. 55.

Chapter 6

Page 60, line 3: Ibid., p. 48.

Page 61, line 3: *Memoirs of Socrates and the Symposium (The Dinner Party),* p. 15–16.

Page 62, line 17: *The Trials of Socrates: Six Classic Texts by Plato, Aristophanes, and Xenophon,* p. 48.

Chapter 7

Page 66, line 8: *Memoirs of Socrates and the Symposium (The Dinner Party),* p. 9.

Page 66, line 21: *The Trials of Socrates: Six Classic Texts by Plato, Aristophanes, and Xenophon,* p. 37.

Page 68, line 16: Ibid., p. 184.

Page 70, line 22: Ibid., p. 4.

Page 71, line 4: Ibid., p. 5.

Chapter 8

Page 75, line 16: *The Trials of Socrates: Six Classic Texts by Plato, Aristophanes, and Xenophon,* pp. 35–36.

Page 76, line 19: Ibid., p. 46.

Page 77, line 20: Ibid., p. 45.

Page 78, line 7: Ibid., p. 54.

Page 79, line 23: Ibid., p. 61.

Chapter 9

Page 81, line 7: Ibid., p. 62.

Page 81, line 9: Ibid.

Page 82, line 24: Ibid., p. 63.

Page 83, line 12: Ibid., pp. 64–65.

Page 84, line 1: Ibid., p. 78.

Page 84, line 7: Ibid.

Page 87, line 13: Plato. *Phaedo* (trans. R. Hackforth). Cambridge, UK.: Cambridge University Press, 1955, pp. 105–106.

Page 87, line 26: Ibid., pp. 94–95.

Page 88, line 4: Ibid., p. 95.

Page 89, line 4: *The Trials of Socrates: Six Classic Texts by Plato, Aristophanes, and Xenophon,* p. 79.

Page 89, line 8: Ibid.

Page 89, line 10: Ibid.

Page 90, line 7: Ibid.

Page 91, line 16: Ibid., p. 80.

Page 91, line 19: Ibid., p. 81.

Page 91, line 25: Ibid.

Page 92, line 6: Ibid., p. 82.

Page 92, line 26: Ibid.

Page 93, line 18: Ibid., pp. 82–83.

Page 93, line 30: Ibid., p.83.

Page 95, line 4: *Memoirs of Socrates and the Symposium (The Dinner Party),* p. 11.

Select Bibliography

Adkins, Lesley, and Roy A. Adkins. *Handbook to Life in Ancient Greece.* New York: Oxford University Press, 1998.

Cooper, John M., ed. *Complete Works/Plato.* Indianapolis: Hackett Publishing, 1997.

Cornford, Francis Macdonald. M. *Before and After Socrates.* Cambridge, UK.: Cambridge University Press, 1932 (1999 printing).

Diogenes Laertius. *Lives of Eminent Philosophers* (trans. R.D. Hicks). London: W. Heinemann: Putnam, 1925.

Linder, Douglas. "The Trial of Socrates." University of Missouri–Kansas City School of Law, 2002. 3 Feb. 2006. www.law.umkc.edu/faculty/projects/ftrials/socrates/socratesaccount.html

Nails, Debra. "Socrates." *The Stanford Encyclopedia of Philosophy* (Fall 2005). Edward N. Zalta. ed. 3 Feb. 2006.www.plato.stanford.edu/entries/socrates/

Plato. *Phaedo* (trans. R. Hackforth). Cambridge, UK.: Cambridge University Press, 1955.

Plato. *The Last Days of Socrates* (trans. Hugh Tredennick and Harold Tarrant). London: Penguin Books, 2003.

Plato. *The Trial and Death of Socrates: Four Dialogues* (trans. Benjamin Jowett). New York: Dover Publications, 1992.

Plato. *The Trial and Death of Socrates.* 3rd ed. (trans. G.M.A. Grube). Indianapolis: Hackett Publishing, 2000.

Reeve, C.D.C., ed. *The Trials of Socrates: Six Classic Texts by Plato, Aristophanes, and Xenophon.* Indianapolis: Hackett Publishing, 2002.

Stone, I.F. "I.F. Stone Breaks the Socrates Story: An Old Muckraker Sheds Fresh Light on the 2,500-Year-Old Mystery and Reveals Some Athenian Political Realities That Plato Did His Best to Hide." *New York Times Magazine,* 8 April 1979: 22.

Stone, I.F. *The Trial of Socrates.* New York: Anchor Books, 1989.

Vlastos, Gregory, ed. *The Philosophy of Socrates: A Collection of Critical Essays.* Notre Dame, Ind.: University of Notre Dame Press, 1980.

Xenophon. *Memoirs of Socrates and the Symposium (The Dinner Party)* (trans. Hugh Tredennick). Harmondsworth, UK.: Penguin Books, 1970.

Pamela Dell began her professional career writing for adults and started writing for children about 12 years ago. Since then she has published fiction and nonfiction books, written numerous magazine articles, and created award-winning interactive multimedia.